After The Rain

there is always a rainbow

After The Rain

there is always a rainbow

JACQUI DELORENZO, MS

ReadersMagnet, LLC

After The Rain: There is Always a Rainbow
Copyright © 2021 by Jacqui DeLorenzo, MS

Published in the United States of America
ISBN Paperback: 978-1-955603-56-0
ISBN eBook: 978-1-955603-55-3

All rights reserved. No part of this publication may be reproduced, stored in a retrieval system or transmitted in any way by any means, electronic, mechanical, photocopy, recording or otherwise without the prior permission of the author except as provided by USA copyright law.

The opinions expressed by the author are not necessarily those of ReadersMagnet, LLC.

ReadersMagnet, LLC
10620 Treena Street, Suite 230 | San Diego, California, 92131 USA
1.619.354.2643 | www.readersmagnet.com

Book design copyright © 2021 by ReadersMagnet, LLC. All rights reserved.
Cover design by Kent Gabutin
Interior design by Renalie Malinao

CONTENTS

Book Reviews ix
Life Has Many Changes and Life Goes On!. xi
Appreciation xiii
Acknowledgments xv
Special Thoughts and Blessings xvii
Introduction xix
Dedication xxi
Special remembrance xxiii
Preface xxv

Chapter One 1
Chapter Two 5
Chapter Three 9
Chapter Four 14
Chapter Five 21
Chapter Six 27
Chapter Seven 33
Chapter Eight 39
Chapter Nine 44
Chapter Ten 47

Epilogue 55

May the Angels always carry you on their wings!!

Please check out my website:
jacquidelorenzo.com

May your life be blessed with everything beautiful!
Be happy you are only here once so make the best of it.

Be Happy

BOOK REVIEWS

Once again, Jacqui does not disappoint. She shares intimate stories told in an inspiring manner. She keeps the reader engaged in her personal stories told in a straight from the heart way. This book is a wonderful gift. Like Jacqui and her faith in God, this book reminds us, as in the title, "After the Rain-always a Rainbow.

Marilyn Nagle

Devoted followers of Jacqui DeLorenzo, author of A Thread of Hope and Straight from the heart have been eagerly awaiting her third book, After the Rain, There is Always a Rainbow. This next installment in a series of books is designed to strengthen the soul through this dark time of the COVID-19 pandemic of 2020-2021. In her usual way, Jacqui demonstrates how to dig deep within our being and find ways to reframe our fears and lack of hope; to become the conqueror versus the victim. Readers are treated to poignant stories and corresponding poems that will lift our dampened spirits to truly see the "rainbow" in all aspects of our lives. This book is a must for these challenging times! –

Jennifer McCarthy, EdD, EdM, MS, LCPC

"After the Rain: There is always a Rainbow" is a wonderful collection of powerful memoirs of overcoming difficult times. Beautiful poetry and suggestions for the reader to reframe your thinking and preserve through difficult times. This book is a recommended uplifting inspirational read.

Ellen Ernst

Jacqui DeLorenzo is a shining example that the Rainbow always comes after the rain, no matter how bad the storm. She has created a life blessing even as she has experienced tragedies along the way. She continues to spread the message to others: hold on to hope and grey skies will turn blue.

Kirsten Manville

LIFE HAS MANY CHANGES AND LIFE GOES ON!

Since the publication of "Straight from my Heart: Journeys of Hope, Love, and Peace" many things have changed for me. Some are very positive and some not so positive. However, I have always kept my faith and the hope KNOWING that my savior Jesus will always help me through whatever life has tossed my way. My spiritual faith has been my survival. The angels have always been close by and I thank God for them especially my guardian angel, whom I named Angel. (Priscilla)

I left the college that I was working at as a full-time LMHC/Academic counselor. I still work part-time but with this pandemic coronavirus, I have stepped back for a while. I fill my time taking care of my two adorable nephews.

Jayden is age 5 years old and Dominic a little over a year. They are my life and add joy to my day. My niece Ashleigh and Joshua have included me in their family as a member and I am so grateful. I also have another two nephews Gregory and Jason and a niece, Melissa. They are precious and add to my world too.

I lost my best friend, my mom. I love her so much. We were the best of pals. She had several small strokes. She always kept her sense of humor until the very end when she had another stroke that left her unable to communicate in any way. She was 96 years old; I miss her so much. I know she is around me, but I miss her physical body and her presence. I miss my mom, my best friend. She will always be by my side.

I lost my dear sister Debbie. She passed away from lung cancer at 61 years of age. She never smoked a day in her life and lived a good healthy life. She never did get to see her grandchildren, but she did know that she was going to be a grandmother. Lung cancer is horrible like any other cancer. I miss her so much. She was so kind, so sweet, and ever so caring.

I have had some obstacles in my life which haven't been great, but I am a survivor and making it through with the help of God. I lost most of my hearing in my right ear due to a virus that I got from a very bad cold. It is difficult getting used to hearing with one ear, but I am so grateful that I can still hear. I thank God for that.

I also got sick and ended up in the hospital for nine days and got diagnosed with Congestive Heart Failure and AFIB. AFIB is a heart condition that affects the way the heart pumps. I am on medication that helps. I don't let this condition stand in my way. I do whatever I had done before I still exercise at a great health club, help my niece, and still see my friends, and I continue to write. In other words, I keep active. I have always strived to be a conqueror and not a victim. We have that choice.

Life is never perfect, and life changes all the time. It is up to us to adjust to the changes good and bad. We live in a changing world and a world that throws out many positive things along with not so positive. Remember keep the faith and "Never give up!"

APPRECIATION

Hi, Blessings to all of you!

When my phone rang, I saw it was *Readers Magnet*. Although I never answer the phone unless I know who it is, I answered. Why? I didn't know at the time, but I know now. A gentleman from a self-publishing company introduced himself as Victor. In my mind, I said to myself "oh boy he is going to try to have me invest in his company." He had a lot to share with me and how *Readers Magnet* would work for me. He was kind, sincere, and no pressure or stress. A month later I got the call from Kyle Torrez from Readers Magnet. He explained how Victor had to leave and he would be taking his place. Kyle was kind, sincere, more than helpful, and very informative. He never has pressured me. This is what I feared the most. He has shared ideas, suggestions, views, and thoughts on how my books being revised would be more viewable and more appealing to the general public. He has helped me with every step of the way, and he did not degrade or make me feel inadequate in any way.

Kyle, unfortunately, had to leave Readers Magnet which worried me. However, he got replaced by super individuals that continued to help me: Rain and Ryza. They were both terrific. The Financial Department was also very nice along with the editing department, etc. Everyone was wonderful.

I could not suggest any better self-publishing company than Readers Magnet. "I love Readers Magnet." I am thrilled and I have never felt more confident in spreading hope, peace, and comfort to all of you. Blessings to all of you.

Never give up, there is always hope, even if it is just "A Thread of Hope".

ACKNOWLEDGMENTS

Special Thank you to my dear friend, **Therese "Terri" Kay.** She is an author herself and has helped me tremendously with this book. I invite you to check out her website: www.theresekay.com.

I would like to send out a special thank you to my dear friends **Joan and Bob Peabody.** Their computer skills help was outstanding, and I could not thank them enough. Their kindness and willingness to help me are always there for me and because of them, I could proceed with what I love most.

Special thank you to **Bob Murphy** who is so amazing in his computer skills. His patience deserves an award.

Thank you to **Readers Magnet** and the wonderful consultants that helped me through this process. **Victor, Kyle, Rain, Ryza, Bob and Arlene**, and all of the Readers Magnet staff.

Thank you to my Readers **Jennifer McCarthy, Marilyn Nagle, Ellen Ernst, and Kirsten Manville.**

SPECIAL THOUGHTS AND BLESSINGS

Blessings and love to my **sister Jeanne** and my **brother-in-law John**.

Blessings and love to my very special **Uncle Bert**. His love for our Lord Jesus blesses him with great wisdom and love.

Blessings and love to my dear **Aunt (Trudy) Gert Nielsen**

Blessings to my **Aunt Barbara DeLorenzo**

Special love and hugs to all my **dear friends** who have always stuck beside me. I would mention you but if I forgot one of you I would feel terrible. You know who you are. Thank you so much.

A very special grateful appreciation for the love I have in my heart for **my Savior Jesus**. I could not live without him by my side every day. He is my strength, my wisdom, my love. He has guided me, and He protects me.

A very special thank you to his **Blessed mother Mary.**

Thank you to **my guardian angel, Angel** (Priscilla), and all the **angels, Archangels, and Saints** who have always remained by my side with their protection and love.

A special thank you to my niece **Ashleigh** and **Josh** for including me as part of their family with my beautiful nephews Jayden and Dominic who have made my life worth living.

INTRODUCTION

Does it ever stop raining?

Sometimes when you think you made it through, another storm hits you in the face. No one ever said that life would be easy. This sounds like a negative way to start a book. I know it is supposed to be uplifting. It is! It is reality and it is called life with all its ups and downs. So now that we have gotten reality out of the way let's see how we choose to deal with it.

You can choose to be a **conqueror or a victim!** You and only you have that choice. Life today deals with us well and badly. 10% is what happens, but 90% is how we make the situation positive. It is our choice.

Amen!

DEDICATION

I dedicate this book to my beautiful great-nephews and great-nieces. I wish them a beautiful life full of Hope, Love, Health, and Peace. They live in a brand-new world, to say the least, and I wish them a healthy life. Most of all I wish them to always have God in their hearts and always believe that there is life beyond this one. I hope they believe and hold on to their guardian angel that God gave them the day they were born. I pray and hope that they believe their angel will help, guide, and protect them.

My beautiful and loving nieces and nephews: **Christine, John, Ashleigh, Meaghan, and Brandon**

My great-nephews: **Gregory, Jason, Jayden, Dominic**

And to my great-niece **Melissa**

I give you all my love. I pray you have great wisdom and you always have a love for others and yourself. Always remember the Golden rule. Treat others as you would like to be treated. Jesus loves you.

SPECIAL REMEMBRANCE

Special love and remembrance to my mom, **Anita C. DeLorenzo**. We will always be the best of buddies. Special love to all my loved ones in heaven including my dad **John DeLorenzo**, my grandmothers, grandfathers, all my aunts, uncles, and friends.

PREFACE

I hope you enjoy my new book **"After the Rain" There Is Always a Rainbow."**

I want to instill in you that there is always hope and there is always an answer. We are truly blessed. This book holds, love, hope, faith, inspiration, encouragement, and a new breath for this "new" world we are about to enter.

Life is a blessing as if we didn't already know that before, we certainly must know now. We have had another tough lesson in life. It is called survival. We must survive!! It is built into our genes and we do this every day of our lives. We have been to the depths of the ocean finding our way out of this pandemic. We are in a very positive way. We will do it!

I can feel in my heart and in my soul a breath of fresh air… clean, fresh air. Doesn't that sound wonderful? We now have vaccines, and we are getting vaccinated. We are going to get rid of this devil that lives amongst us and it will feel our wrath. God is good and He has given the doctors and the scientist the knowledge to create powerful vaccines. A huge thanks to all the others behind the scenes.

Set your sites on a beautiful new year. Barbecues or (cookouts) to us in New England, eating outside, inside with our loved ones and friends, going to movies, concerts, etc. We can walk on a beach without a mask and breathe the fresh air. BUT most of all we can be with family and friends. We can hug them, and we can kiss them, we can see them. We can all be happy and we all can be safe. God bless America and the world. Amen.

Somewhere over the Rainbow

Somewhere over the rainbow as I look into the sky,
I see so many colors that my eyes begin to shine.
Each color has its special meaning just let me start to tell
The beauty of each every color will brighten up the sun.

Look at that bright Red it speaks for itself
It's the first color of the rainbow and oh so beautiful.
Orange lives next to red it shines itself on its own.
We have this soft Yellow that seems to warm our hearts.
And then we have the color Green reminds us of the trees.
Blue is such a soft warm color that warms our mighty soul
And then its friend Indigo that is told to be very bold.
The beauty of the Purple that is so sensitive and warm
Just finish the beauty of the rainbow that tells us life goes on.

CHAPTER ONE

Open your heart and let the love flow in for love is pure and beautiful.

Hope is Alive

I have talked about Hope so many times because for me and all of you **Hope** is what we hang on to. We have prayed and we hoped that a vaccine would be found to cure this pandemic that we are now living in. Well, our prayers are answered and our hope became a reality. In fact, at this point, we now have three vaccines. Praise God for the wonderful doctors and scientists who have worked diligently in finding a cure. I am very optimistic. I see a beautiful bright light about to shine upon us. I am vaccinated and I have such comfort inside of me. So today I am thankful, grateful, appreciative, and blessed. I wish all of you the great faith I have in this vaccine. I wish health, peace, happiness, and love. I wish us all wisdom to have learned from this experience and a great journey in our brand-new world.

Hope

I hope you are well and enjoying life to the fullest. Life can be tough and not easy at times. Life happens and we have no control over many things that interrupt our lives. The one thing we do have control over is how we handle it. We have a choice to be the conqueror or be the victim. We can look at life and be thankful for all the things we have and count our blessings or go to a dark place and say, "Why me"?

When you think about it the decision should come easy. It is a better place to be with a positive view of how we can handle our everyday situations. I choose to be a conqueror. I think I have always felt that way and believe me, it hasn't always been the easiest, but it has always been the best route for me to travel. Life as they say, "It is what it is." So, I am going to share two life experiences that just recently happened to me. It isn't the worst in the world, but it happened to me and I have to deal with it being a conqueror all the way.

Life #1

One was the death of my very best friend in the entire world. My mom. My mom was my best friend. Even growing up as a child and through my teens, my mom was the best. She was the best mom ever and she was always there for me. As I got older, we would travel together, go shopping, dine, and help each other whenever needed. She was my soulmate. I knew that chances were that she would probably pass before me. I used to imagine living without my best friend to try to help myself when the day came. However, I would not let my mind go there because my heart would take over. My brain knew it was a reality. My heart knew it would become unbelievably painful.

The day would come soon enough, and it did. On September 8th, 2019, my mom passed away at 96. My mom was loved by many and the "She lived a good long life", so sorry for your loss", you were so lucky to have her" came rolling in through cards, visits, phone calls, and more. I knew that, and people meant well but my heart was broken but not beyond repair. I knew I could do it. I just needed her again to help me through this terrible loss. I know you never get over losing someone, but you do learn to live with the loss. Again, I did grieve, and I still grieve but I remember the good times. I feel her in my heart and my soul and I know she will never leave me.

Our body is just a casing, but our true selves are our souls. A soul never dies. The soul carries everyone they ever loved and everyone who ever loved them. So, they never truly leave you. If you can believe this it truly helps you through the days that are sometimes difficult. You will see them again and that is my belief. I hope you can think about this and I hope it helps you with a loved one you may have lost. Everyone needs to find a special way to cope. It is different for everyone. No one lived or lives your life, so no one knows but you what works the best. Writing a blog for me can sometimes be difficult in various ways. It can be very emotional.

Life #2

This was the loss of hearing in one of my ears due to an ear infection that turned into a virus. As a result, I have 8% hearing in my ear. I remember answering the phone one day and I couldn't hear anything. At first, I thought it was the phone not working correctly. I kept saying hello, hello, but could not hear a response. I put the phone to my other ear and could hear the person on the other end of the landline. This frightened me. I wasn't sure what was happening, but I was certainly going to find out. I made an appointment with my primary care. She checked my ears for wax, ear infection, whatever she could do. She said she was concerned and thought I should see an audiologist. My doctor sent me to an ear doctor and audiologist. After an intense exam, I was told that I got a virus that deafened me in one ear. It was irreversible and my hearing would not come back. This was a real blow to me. I did not believe what I was hearing (no pun intended). I couldn't believe that one day I could hear perfectly and the next day I had been diagnosed with hearing loss. After many tests and exams by the doctor, the result was deafness and I should go to the audiologist for hearing aids, I thought boy how is this going to work, will I be able to hear like before?

I saw the audiologist. She gave me hearing aids to try and to see if they could help at all. Well, I did get the hearing aids. Can I hear like before? Not! The clarity is often distorted, and it is difficult to hear especially at a restaurant and with a group of people. I would say the only time I can hear without too much difficulty is if I am alone with a friend and they are directly in front of me when they are talking. So, this hasn't been easy, and it has been a real adjustment for me. However, I looked closely at my situation and again I tell myself "it is what it is", So Jacqui, how are you going to handle this one. Again, my choice. Be a conqueror or slip into "poor me." I still have hearing in one ear. I could have lost hearing in both ears. I consider myself blessed.

So, again life never promised us a rose garden, but we can choose to pick the flowers or the weeds in the garden of life.

Blessings to all my friends. May the angels always carry you on their wings.

CHAPTER TWO

*May you always be guided by The Holy Spirit
and may his light shine down on you always*

A Miracle Has Happened

Whether you believe in miracles or not there is something extraordinary! I am a believer in miracles so for me this is miraculous. We now have a positive, effective, safe vaccine. This has been a year, not even a year that has tested our hope, faith, love, endurance, patience, mindfulness, and all the words that may come to you now. I know some of you are reading this wondering why I have so much confidence in this. I believe in science and I truly believe that through God's guidance and the millions of people that have been praying for this cure that our prayers are answered. This is the new beginning for us. So, the dark tunnel that we all have been traveling with a dim light is opening up a bright light, a new beginning, and a brand-new world for us to live in. The key is what have we learned from this. We have learned a lot, and this is one of the biggest lessons we probably have ever endured. We will live in a "new" world but a better world. We will be more aware, conscientious, grateful, appreciative, and thankful. We will be more careful about how we take care of ourselves and others. We will love it more. I love you all. May the angels guide you and surround you and all your loved ones.

Straight from My Heart

I hope you enjoy this chapter because it is "Straight from my heart." This is the title of my second book that was truly written from my heart. If you were never a believer in life beyond this world you may feel a flicker or become a true believer that there is life after this one. If you are a believer this will be a true page-turner for you. Open your hearts for those who at this point. Can you imagine knowing that the ones you loved you will see again?

I always tell myself that one of these days I am going to write a book that has inspirational poems and thoughts and include my friend's poems and thoughts. I think many people do not like to read long stories or books. I think if I wrote a book sharing life's stories and such many would be able to connect in this way. I always loved poems. They were quick and easy and said what they had to say. Believe it or not, I am not an avid reader myself, but I do like quick reads. I think that is why many of you like reading my books because I try to keep my writing easy to read. So, having said that I will continue my writing in a way that you can all relate to. I want you to feel as I am talking to you.

The books I write are from my heart. I have had some tell me that when they read my books it is like we are having a conversation. We are just talking as friends. I am not the best writer for sure, but I do the best I can. I have dyslexia so excuse me if I mess up a bit. My main concern is getting my love and message to you to let you know you are not alone and that someone truly cares about you. You are never alone, and you always have someone by your side either here on earth or some loved one that has passed before you.

Each of my chapters is different in most senses. My story is not one story but different stories. If you have read some of the things I say before just know that they relate to the story I am telling. Life entwines and we all have a connection.

Please enjoy my outreach to you and know that I do care, and I hope you will find comfort because my stories are straight from my heart and I treasure the gift of being able to spread my word out to you.

It has been a tough time this past year and we have the entire world working to make it better. There is a lot better in the world than evil. We are fighting evil and we will win!

Our beautiful world was hit with a "bomb." We never did expect this, nor did we ever have such a blow to our entire world since 1918 with the Spanish flu. We hardly ever looked at that because it never really concerned us. We never realized what those poor innocent people went through. It was devastating. In the year 1918, they didn't have the medical expertise we have today. They panicked, rightfully so. They didn't know what to do, where to go or what was going to happen to their world. It is very scary to us while we are going through with Covid 19. So, you can only imagine what they were thinking. We always have hope. Looking back, it seems like this virus has been around for years, but it has only been around for months, as I write this today, not even a year. It is funny though that although it feels like years the time still goes by so quickly for most of us, I should say. I keep telling myself this will end, and we will go back to a new world but a very accepting, grateful world. We will be able to go back to work, have dinner at restaurants with our family and friends, we will go back to all our "normal activities" that were taken away from us. We will travel without fear, we will be able to visit freely. We will go to Libraries, go to concerts, go to the movies and much more. Most of all we will be able to see our families, see our friends, and we will be able to hug them, kiss them love them. We took all this for granted and we have learned from it. It's a brand-new world for us. Let's enjoy every minute. Let's thank God for a new chance to live our lives differently and be so thankful that we who survived Covid 19 have that chance. God Bless America and the world around us.

CHAPTER THREE

How I love and miss you with every beat of my heart

Catch a Star

We can reach for a star and grab onto it. Look up at the sky it is beautiful and has so much to offer. It is an endless sky with millions of stars twinkling at us. It is telling us there is life, beautiful life. We should all be looking up with hope, love, faith, and determination. We all must move forward keeping our eyes minds, souls looking up. We don't want to stay in a darkened world. When we look down, we see dirt and holes. We fall in. The longer we look down the more we get stuck and more difficult it is to release ourselves from it. We live in a beautiful world that is going through a crisis, but it is not the end, but it is a new beginning. We are learning so much from this and we will be a better world because we will each be a better person. We have learned and still learning. We will look at this "new world" with a new view on how we look at ourselves, our country our world. God Bless you, America, and the world. Amen.

Debbie, Losing the Best

Since the publication of "Straight from my Heart: Journeys of Hope, Love, and Peace" many things have changed for me. Some are very positive and some not so positive. However, I have always kept the faith and the hope KNOWING that my savior Jesus will always help me through whatever life has tossed my way. My spiritual faith has been my survival. The angels have always been close by and I thank God for them especially my guardian angel, whom I named Angel. (Priscilla)

I left the college that I was working at as a full-time LMHC/Academic counselor. I still work part-time but with this pandemic coronavirus, I have stepped back for a while. I fill my time in by taking care of my two adorable nephews. They are Jayden age 5 years old and Dominic a year and a half. They are my life and add joy to my day. My niece Ashleigh and Joshua have included me as a member of their family and I am so grateful.

Again, I could not forget my two nephews Gregory and Jason, and a niece Melissa. They are precious and add to my world too.

I lost my dear sister Debbie. She passed away from lung cancer at 61 years of age. She never smoked a day in her life and lived a good healthy life. She never did get to see her grandchildren, but she did know that she was going to be a grandmother. Lung cancer is horrible like any other cancer. I miss her so much.

My sister Debbie and I were super close and we shared many secrets. We helped each other all the time. She was a great listener and she always confided in me in her tough times. How could I even comprehend the thought of losing her to this horrendous disease called the big "C" -- cancer!

My sister Debbie was kind, considerate, loving, caring, and giving; plus all the adjectives that one could muster up. It was a total shock when she was diagnosed with stage four lung cancer.

The worst news was that her cancer was incurable. She was given less than a year to live. Our family could not believe it. This was a nightmare and we wanted to wake up from this horror. It was the end of August 2014 and we were invited to a wedding of her daughter's best friend. The occasion was joyous. It was at a beautiful place called Danversport Yacht Club. Of course, my sister Debbie did everything she could to help make her friend's wedding reception the best. It was a glorious wedding reception. During the reception, a friend asked her to dance. Of course, she obliged. Debbie could not make it through the dance. Debbie's breathing got worse. She didn't know what was happening. She couldn't breathe. I am not an alarmist, but this was a red flag.

She made an appointment to see the doctor that week. The doctor seemed overly concerned. She sent my sister for tests. The news was devastating. Cancer. The very worst of it was she had stage 4 lung cancer. "Incurable." This was devastating news.

They gave my sister Debbie one year to live. So where do you even begin knowing this? Well for one thing we told ourselves it is not going to happen, and we began to pray. We prayed and prayed. My sister Jeanne and I helped her children the best we could take my sister to all her treatments. I stayed with her for a while helping her out in any way I could. My sister Debbie and I would end the night with us praying to Jesus, and all who would help her. One night she said to me, "Jacqui, do you smell Pa's cigar?" (Pa) was our grandfather who had passed in 1977. I said no I don't smell anything. She said, "It is so strong!" I knew it was my grandfather connecting with her. Although this was amazing it was also enlightening. My heart told me that it would not be long before a loved one in heaven would be taking her by the hand to lead her into a new world. My sister's guardian angel would lead her there on her wings. My sister named her angel Gabriella.

It is said that you will get some connection with the other world just before you are going to pass into it. I knew the end was near and I knew my sister Debbie knew this also. We always believed in this and now we were seeing it come true. As sad as it was to me, I felt so close to God. It was proof even more that life does go on and there is a more beautiful world that we will all enter at some time. I am not afraid to pass. I think it will be beautiful, welcoming, and so peaceful. Not believing in this would be so sad for me. To think I would not see my loved ones ever again would be so very painful for me to even think.

I hope you all can feel the love of your guardian angel. You all have one and you can give her/him a name. It is a beautiful thing, and you will find comfort in knowing they are there to guide and protect you.

Not long after that did my sister entered a Hospice house. She was only there a day and a half. She passed away from a blood clot. My niece got a call on that Wednesday morning. After the devastating passing of my beloved sister Debbie in August 2015 six months later we were blessed with the birth of my adorable precious nephew Jayden. He was to be my sister Debbie's first grandchild. She always wanted to have grandchildren. She would have made the best Grammy in the world. I often say that if she were still with us physically, I probably would not even know Jayden as I do today or Dominic. (Only kidding, well maybe not) I know I would have had to fight over them. God works in mysterious ways because I believed he blessed me with Jayden and Dominic.

I care for Dominic and Jayden to help their "mommy" Ashleigh. Jayden and Dominic love going to this playhouse called "Room to Bloom." Originally Children's Piazza. It is a fantastic place for kids. It is a fantastic place for adults. The area is set up with a half wall that allows parents time to sit have coffee and a snack while watching their kids play. Of course, parents can join their kids at any time or watch the children no matter where they are in the house but large enough for them to play. They have a ball room with a small rock-climbing wall, a training room, a dark room that brightly lights up with magnetic toys, and a building set. It also has a room for children who do not walk yet and can play or just hang out. There is a large room that has four different height slides, swings, kitchen, trampoline, and more. Jayden and Dominic both love it. I feel so close to my sister and I know that she is thrilled that I am helping my niece and brother-in-law. As I hold Jayden and Dominic in my heart, I hold my sister Debbie.

CHAPTER FOUR

*I wish you love in your heart, peace in your soul,
and happiness in your life.*

You Can Always Find Joy

Last week was my mom's first anniversary (September 8th, 2019 of her passing to her new life in heaven. It was also my brother Johnny's birthday in heaven. He was only 13 years old when he passed away from leukemia many years ago. My sister and I brought my mom a beautiful red plant and my brother a white rose. My mom loved the color red and my brother's pure spirit made the rose a perfect addition to where their casing lay to rest. It was a touching week with many beautiful memories that we remembered as we "talked" to them during our visit. Although we miss them so much at times, we chose to find joy in our visit. Even though their loss was so sad we knew in our hearts that the casing was gone and that their soul lived. The joy in our journey was the beautiful memories and thoughts that no one could take away from us. The joy in knowing that they were no longer suffering and that they were happy with all the ones they loved and the ones who loved them. The joy was knowing that they are happy in the arms of Jesus and free of all their pain. The joy is that they are joyous, happy, content, and peaceful. How could one not feel the Joy?

Mom in Heaven

I always believed in a soul. Our body is just a casing and within it lies who we truly are. So today more than ever I remind myself of my belief. A body dies with all of its imperfections, but our soul passes a distinct difference. A soul carries with it everyone they ever loved and everyone who ever loved them. What a beautiful thing to know. I know my mom will always be around and will never forget those she loved and those who loved her.

My mom was an amazing woman. My mom's life speaks for itself. She was strong, she was courageous, tenacious to say the least, and a very nice woman. People would always tell my sisters and me how sweet my mom was. Our reply would always be: You didn't have her for a mother. She was extremely strict. Even at 21 years old still living at home we had to abide by the rules. If we weren't home, we would pay the price…just ask my sister Jeanne. However, it paid off. We grew up to be responsible, respectable, caring individuals who were taught to treat others like we want to be treated.

We always loved my mom. We may not have always liked her, but we always loved her. You know why? We knew that she always loved us. She brought up four children on her own and never once strayed away from us. We never went to bed hungry and never went to bed cold. We didn't have much money, but we were wealthy in the ways that matter.

All of our friends loved my mom, and many would call her mom. She was indeed a mom to many. My mom was a conqueror.

My mom had many losses. My sister Mary died at 5 days old. I remember even though I was only 7 years old my mom coming home empty-handed with no baby. A room filled with baby gifts; a nursery all set up with no baby to lay in the crib. My mom went into a deep depression, so my grandmother came to live with us for a while until my mom was able to care for us. When my brother was 12 years old three days before his thirteenth birthday, he was diagnosed with leukemia. The news was grim. In 1973 children with leukemia didn't usually survive. The death rate was around 96%. He was just fine three days before he got diagnosed. He had just had his physical before going back into school. The worst possible news a mother could ever hear with a diagnosis of terminal.

One week into his illness he was lying in his hospital bed. He put out his arms stretching toward the ceiling and stated that Jesus was telling him to come to him. It was as if we got hit by lightning. We went to the chapel and prayed Jesus would not take him. Not our Johnny…my mom was only 49 years old. Johnny did survive for nine months before Jesus took him home. Again, my mom survived a devastating loss always keeping her faith. She never got over losing our Johnny. I don't believe you ever do. I believe you learn to live with the loss but never truly get over the loss. You live with a broken heart.

My mom has had many illnesses but always kept a smile and looked at life through gratefulness instead of "why me" syndrome. As I said she was a conqueror and would fight until the end.

Our sister Debbie was her sunshine. However, our sister Debbie grew up in a different house figuratively speaking. By the time she was born curfews had gone out the window. My mom either got with the times or just got tired of saying no. My sister turned out okay, more than ok, she was the best mom, daughter, sister, and friend anyone could ever ask for. Everyone loved our Debbie. I feel when my sister Debbie passed away from lung cancer at the age of 61 my mom shut down. Her heart was shattered and there was no way to heal her heart. Even though all this her faith in Jesus sustained her but the emptiness inside would not let her go. How does anyone ever survive so many losses and still be able to smile? My mom did.

So, my mom was left with the two of us. My loving sister Jeanne and me.

The most difficult decision my sister Jeanne and I had to make was realizing that my mom needed total care. The painful reality was that we had to admit to ourselves that we could not provide that care to her and that it was a safety issue. A nursing home was the only answer. A painful decision. I reflect on how my mom was in her prime and even into her 90's. She held on to her tenacity, her strength, her love of life, and her love for her family and friends. She just wouldn't let go.

A great example that many of you know about my mom is this cute little story. A true story. This is a typical mom.

After a weekend, my colleagues and I would always share what we did. So, I shared the story of how my mom and I went to New Hampshire for a ride, shop at the Walmart up in Seabrook, and then finish the day at the 99 with dinner and our glass of Beranger's(White Zinfandel.) Many told us that this was baby wine, but we loved it.

One of my colleagues said:

"Aren't you nice to spend time with your mom and take her for a nice drive up to New Hampshire?"

My reply was. "Heck no, she took me!"

She was in her late 80's at the time. My mom loved to drive, and she always insisted on driving. That's my excuse. Why would I deprive her of that? I didn't like to drive anymore so this was perfect.

My sisters and I would always call her on her cell phone to see how she was and if she were ok. She would always be okay and never at home. More than once when we called, she would say that she was just shopping and enjoying it. "So where are you, Mom?" She would state that she was at Walmart, for example. Oh, in Salem? "No" she would reply in Seabrook…New Hampshire. She also would love to get lost to find new roads. She was very adventurous and very tenacious. My mom was a great driver. Remember, I was the passenger in the passenger seat in the front.

Everyone considered her Sweet Anita, except her daughters… she was nice but as kids, we didn't consider her sweet. My sisters and I would always laugh about that. One thing for sure you did not want to mess with my mom. My sisters and I would know first handedly.

My mom had all these funny sayings. My mother had this saying: "In the pigs nocuous"! What is a pig's nocuous…does anyone know?

She had other sayings too, but I will hold off on them.

My mom's legacy will live forever. My mom was my soulmate. She is my soulmate. I miss her with my entire being. I will never be whole again. She took a big part of my heart and soul. You never get over losing someone, however, you learn to live with the loss. I know this because I have done it many times in the past.

On behave of my sister Jeanne and I there are no words that could thank all of you for all the love you gave to my mom through the years. Some special people were always in her life and because I know I would forget someone I will just say you know who you are.

I know my mom is here today in Spirit and I'm just waiting for the lights to flicker or something because I feel her presence.

When my mom passed on September 8. 2019. I was sitting beside her with my sister, and my niece Meaghan. I remember she opened her eyes briefly, looked up into the sky, gave one big smile, closed her eyes, and took her last breath. I remember thinking before that I would never live through her passing. It would be too devastating for me. She was my best friend, my mom, my confidence. She was everything to me. I loved her more than life itself and she meant everything to me. I ended up with "two" moms in a sense. My new mom lived with me for a while after her stroke before moving into the facility. My mom changed and in the four years that she lived as my new mom I grieved my old mom. When she passed, I grieved my new mom. I know this may sound strange but weirdly it made it easier for me to accept her passing. Along with my immense sorrow, I found comfort that she is no longer in pain. She is free of the sometimes painful world she lived in. I was able to realize that she is now happy and at peace. She is with her loved ones and she is happy.

I thought you might embrace this poem I wrote about our "soul"

The Soul

One never gets over losing someone, but
they learn to live with the loss
For they were so much part of us when
they were here on earth.
A person's soul holds everyone that
they have ever loved and everyone
Who loved them too and so they never leave.
They are by your side day by day
surrounding you with love; they want
You to be happy and also feel their heart.
For one day you will meet again,
and they will greet you at the door
And you will be together again forever and evermore.

> So, when you are feeling lonely
> and feeling quite blue, remember
> That they are near you and loving you so true…

Poetry has always been part of my survival. I would always write poetry as a child, teenager, and adult. I guess everyone must find their way and this was one of mine. I challenge you to try it. You might like it. It helps you think, it inspires you and it gets your feeling out. So, my lasting remarks on "HOPE" are to never let it go and believe that life is worth living and that you truly matter in our world today.

May I end this chapter with my wish for you. I wish you love in your heart, peace in your soul, happiness in your life, but most of all health throughout your life. God Bless.

CHAPTER FIVE

You are never alone, God is always by your side.

Hope

Hope is something without a doubt we all need. Sometimes we feel hopeless but there is always hope even if there is just "A Thread of Hope." In my book "A Thread of Hope: A Woman's Spiritual Journey of Faith from Trauma to Triumph I talk about my journey and my very often struggling through life with just a thread of hope. My life has not been all traumas thank God for that, but it has had intense negatives journeys. I was a thread away from dying, a desperate plea for someone to listen to me. However, even at the depths of my depression, I hung onto the thread. The entire world feels this surreal unhealthy, unsettling world we live in. It isn't an easy world, but we can choose to be a conqueror of it or become a victim of it. Remember we have a choice. For many of us that remember the Twilight Zone, we feel this is where we live right now. I know I do. Let us all look forward. If we look back it holds us back and if we look forward it springs us into a new bright world. We can't change what has happened, but we can make it better. We are on the right track and we are moving fast in the right direction. Many of us have been sick with Covid, many of us know people that have passed, our loved ones, and friends. It is more than sad, but for us, we still have our lives. So why live your life in desperation but instead live with "Hope" one of the best words there is today to live by this is a great sign of hope, a future to rid ourselves of this horrific disease. Don't ever let go of Hope.

Never Give Up Hope

Hope is something without a doubt we all need. Sometimes we feel hopeless but there is always hope even if it is just "A Thread of Hope." In my book "A Thread of Hope: A Woman's Spiritual Journey of Faith from Trauma to Triumph", I talk about my journey and very often struggling through life with just a thread of hope. My life has not been all traumas thank God for that, but it has had intense negative journeys. I was a thread away from dying. I was begging for someone to listen to what I had to say. I was desperate for someone to listen to me. However, even at the depths of my depression, I found a thread of hope to hang on to. If you ever felt this way you are not alone. Never give up. I am glad I didn't. I hope I can give hope to you and raise your spirits and I thank God for every day of my life. Life can be beautiful and you can live in this "beautiful" world if you allow yourself to open your beautiful spirit that is full of positive energy.

The years are 2020/2021. The entire world is going through a terrible pandemic. In our lives, we have never been through a pandemic such as this. This is something we have never experienced in our lifetime. It is so surreal. As I continue to write this book, I ask God that He takes my every stroke of the keys to be a prayer for all of us and I mean all of us, including the world. I often wonder how a "virus" can spread so quickly and be so outrageously contagious. At the moment escaping this virus is minimal. It is in the air. We all wear face masks; we all have to keep at least six feet apart and we must always wash our hands and sanitize continually. We can't see our families and give the usual hugs that we are so accustomed to. This is not ordinary for us and we all find this strange, uncomfortable. I must say for me I always felt thankful for what I had but I never realized at the same time I took whatever I wanted to do for granted. I never thought if I wanted to go somewhere I couldn't just go. I just decided I was going and there was not a problem. Now, I look at life differently and I am thankful. I don't take things for granted and I hope to remember this. I guess this is one of the best lessons I have learned.

For those of you who are a little older, you might remember the Outer Limits, or The Twilight Zone, or One Step Beyond. I feel we are living out of this world like the programs I just mentioned. We have never experienced life like this. However, we will survive this, and we will be stronger. We will appreciate life more than ever. I have to say it is one of the greatest lessons we have ever learned. It is a very good lesson for us. If we learn from this lesson it will leave us with many positive avenues to follow. So, everything has a price. Some of us have paid a price that is beyond imaginable. Some of us are experiencing the loss of our previous lifestyle. It's a memory for now but not an end. We will have a similar life but not the old life. This is good. Some of us have experienced Covid 19 ourselves. Some of us have been very ill and some of us not so ill. We may have a family member or friend or maybe just know someone. I think it is safe to say that we all can relate in some way to Covid 19.

Losing a loved one is the cruelest price one can pay. One positive thing is that we will see that person again. Our body is a casing and our soul lives forever carrying with it everyone they ever loved and everyone who loved them. It doesn't sound that comforting while we are grieving but we can find hope and refuge in knowing this is not the end but a new beginning. Our thoughts can reflect that even though we don't see their physical body (their soul) is indeed around us. I pray daily for the loss that so many have experienced. I know that they are in the best place a person (soul) can be. Again, I must say they are happy so let's be happy for them. They are looking down on all their loved ones and they want us to be happy. They want you to know that they are safe and happy. Most of all they want you to know that you will be with them again someday. They love you. There is no time in heaven, so time is not of importance to them, they are watching over you and believe in your spirit. Always remember they love you and will not leave you.

Many of us have lost our jobs which makes our financial obligations so difficult. This isn't even mentioning the mental state that we all feel. This is reflected in our new world. Schools, colleges, restaurants, stores, health clubs, and entertainment centers, banks, post offices, and the lists continue are a few places that we feel the loss of what they provide without them. Even the doctor's office, dentist office has strict criteria if you can even get an appointment inside the office setting. One group I feel badly about are the seniors in high school, young adults in colleges, eighth grade, and kindergarten that never got to enjoy the joys that come with graduating. This is a once-in-a-lifetime experience for them that they will never enjoy.

The proms, the picnics, the parties and family gatherings, weddings, churches, synagogues, mosques, and other great religious celebrations that for now never took place. However, it is getting better and things are improving. We are going in the right direction. I see the light at the end of the tunnel, and it is not the train.

Again, I always felt thankful for what I had but I didn't know I took it for granted. I was appreciative but I never gave it a thought what it would be to not just live my life like I was so accustomed to. It certainly for me has been an awakening in many ways. I am more thankful than ever! Life is so mysterious because you never know what is around the corner. Taking one step is the best way to travel.

Hope is a very powerful and very strong word. Could you live without "hope"? I know that I could not. It is my lifeline. Hope is the vein that carries us through the most difficult times in our lives. It gives us strength; it sets us free and helps us in everyday life. I think it is one of the most powerful words there is. Again, to me, it is my lifeline. If I didn't have "hope" I would feel lost. I will always have hope even if sometimes it feels like just "a thread of hope" it is always there.

My faith is also my strength. I will always have my savior Jesus in my life. He is my lifeline and what I hang onto. He is my hope. Everyone can find their link. Everyone can find one. I believe in you and I know you all have that link.

With all these losses, interruptions, inconveniences what are we going to do? We will continue picking ourselves up and doing the best we can. We can look ahead, upward, forward, and straight ahead. We now have an effective vaccine. We are looking straight ahead. We can be happy and thankful for all the progress we have made in getting a vaccine for the Covid virus. Hooray, we now have three vaccines!!

A miracle has happened. We can thank the doctors, scientists, pharmacists, and all the medical staff for all their hard work and endless effort in moving this forward. Thank you to all of you who are overlooked. The grocery workers, retail workers, and all those that put their life at risk to help us and make our lives livable and as comfortable as they can be. To end this chapter, we must remember we are on the road to a happy, healthy, peaceful place that we once knew and somehow lost. We are learning a lesson and if we learn from it then we will be at the top of the class. We can wear our masks, wash our hands, and stay a good distance just for now. We will move away from all of this shortly, and we will have big smiles on our faces that we all will be able to see. We will be free!

Thank You, God

Thank you, God, for all you do.
Thank you, God, for all your blessings to us on this earth.
Please stay by our side and guide
Those that need the extra strength in surviving this world.
We thank you, God, with all our heart.

CHAPTER SIX

*May you always feel like a butterfly, free to
fly as you feel God's Grace.*

Coping in Today's World

Coping is a six-letter word with a big meaning. How do you "cope"? It isn't always easy for sure, but we can do it in a very optimistic, positive way. Taking care of yourself is vital. Thinking of others is an important step on our journey to a better world. Having a positive attitude rather than a negative attitude is so important in being able to cope healthily. Remember we have a choice. Thinking about others and their safety is our responsibility when we make our choices. Many things that happen today are beyond our control, but we DO have control over how we are going to handle them. We do have rights and we do have a right to choose. However, I feel if my choice might inflict on others in some way, I need to think clearly about what I choose to do. Peace of mind, heart, and soul is what we all want. We want peace and health in the world and our country, we want our mind to be relaxed and be able to rest our heads on our pillow at night, close our eyes, and sleep. We want our soul to reassure us that things will be better. It will!! We are going in the right direction and the light is beginning to shine. We have hope. We all have love in our hearts, and we need to reach out any way we can. If we have an open mind and keep a positive attitude coping will be easy and we will go with the flow and look for a bright future. Love is the key, hope is the journey, peace, and health on earth are what we strive for. If we think we can, we can. If we think we can't, we can't. I bet I know what you my friends would choose. God bless and God bless America and the world. May the angels always surround you with their guiding light. Blessings Jacqui DeLorenzo.

A New World

We are opening up to a brand-new world. A world where we will make new decisions, choices, and a brand-new way to look and appreciate what we have. I always thought I appreciated life and what God has given to me. I always said thank you and never had I thought took things for granted. Guess what? I was wrong. I realize more than anything now all I did have, and how I took things for granted. I so appreciate things so much more now. I miss going to a restaurant with a friend and sitting where I want, order what I want and feel free to breathe without any real concern. We never had a time limit or a time we had to leave. I never thought twice about going into a movie theater and picking out whatever movie I wanted to see, sit where I wanted to sit and watch the movie with ease and not worry about breathing on someone or someone breathing on me. I never thought twice about jumping in my car with a friend and going to a mall and being able to go into as many stores as I wanted to, also having a coffee at the pavilion, and watching the countless people go by without fear or worry. This is what I took for granted and never realized this is what I did.

I looked forward to a vacation that I had planned and enjoyed the vacation. Again, it was my choice when to go, where to go, how long to go, and just GO. I never looked back or thought about it being canceled I just took it for granted that all would go as planned. So, I went without hesitation and not thinking about anything but to have a good time, relax or not relax and be thankful that I was able to enjoy the vacation but never realized what a gift this was. There is a song by a country singer. Her name is Crystal Gale. She sings about being grateful and appreciative when something you have is taken away how you don't realize how much you are going to miss. One line is:

How much one realizes how appreciative you should be, "A glass of water when the well runs dry." It's a great song. I love country and I always tell my friends who don't, "You have to listen to the words." Every song has a story.

I look back now and realize how very blessed and fortunate I was to have all that I took granted for. I think many of us can relate to this in many ways, this is one avenue that we can pay attention to and turn this horrific virus into a positive lesson. We can learn from this or toss it aside and just become angry and hold the pain in our hearts. We are blessed at this point with the pandemic with at least three vaccines. All the vaccines have been proving to be effective. They are paving the road to building a new highway path to a better life for all. Our world overall within where we live can and will be beautiful again. Patience is a virtue and not always easy to attain. I guess that is why we say "patience is a virtue" lots of thought. We can look at it as a chalkboard. We have erased the evil that has spread across the world and now we have a beautiful clean slate to work with. Each of us has our box of chalk and we can paint our new world in any way we want to.

When you make a mistake and learn from it, it is no longer a mistake. It is a lesson. Remember you have the chalk; you are the captain, and you can draw your new world in any way you want to. If it doesn't seem right erase it and start again. It doesn't matter. Along the way, we may sometimes feel we are losing the battle. This makes us stronger to fight and win the war. Throughout your journey in life remember you are the captain, and you can set your sails in any direction you want to land.

I would like to share this poem with you that was written from my heart. This is a poem that I have in my book "Straight from my Heart." It is one of my favorite poems from the book because it speaks so positive. It gives hope and it gives encouragement. It speaks of the afterlife that awaits us and all the loved ones that are waiting for us. Just remember, heaven has no time so no worry about them missing us. They see us all the time, so time isn't anything to them. We are the ones that must deal with time so think positive and be strong.

Butterflies are one of my favorite creatures that I love. I love everything about butterflies. They are a sign of new life to all of us. They are a breath of fresh air. They give us hope to cling on to and sometimes that is all we have.

BUTTERFLY
(Are free to fly)

Beautiful butterfly, fly by me,
show me your beauty in your
Awesome wings.
Your bright lovely colors show your guiding light,
giving one hope
And faith in the above.
Beautiful butterfly tell us your secret,
you always are happy and

Have a free spirit.
I want to be like you so happy and free,
tell me your secret,
I'm asking you, please.
Beautiful butterfly, are you ready to share?
You know the true answer with one small little prayer.
So beautiful butterfly God's gift from above,
Stay close beside me and show me your love.
Beautiful butterfly beautiful and free,
you are a free spirit that
If one believes.
You will feel the warmth of your
flight beneath your wings,
Oh, beautiful butterfly, you enlighten me.
Stay by my side and guide my way in feeling so positive
Along my way.

Butterflies and angels go together for me. Butterflies are free to fly. They can travel wherever they want to go. I believe butterflies are messages from above. Butterflies are not afraid of us. Butterflies will softly sit on our shoulders if we let them. They are gentle and have manifested into beautiful creatures. Their beautiful wings lift them and they seem to lead positive journeys in their life. I think they know their life is not as long as other friends in their species, so they make the best of their journey here on earth. I believe they were made by God to teach us a lesson that life is shorter than you know so make the most of it. Appreciate your life, don't take things for granted, and live life each day like it was your last day. Life is a lesson. We become stronger from learning what the lesson is teaching us. However, we must be open-minded and be as optimistic as we can in this trying world. Learn from the butterfly. Next time you see a butterfly think about a loved one above. Most likely it is the person who came to your mind. It is they saying hello to you.

They are telling you they are fine, and that life does go on and you will see them again. It is in believing that helps you and it is in believing that gives you hope, strength, and love in your heart.

My new world will be beautiful. My new world will have lots of beautiful colors with gorgeous new views. I shall wake up each morning and give thanks to God for giving me another day. I will be kinder to others, I will share more, love more, care more, and give more. I will be happier, more grateful, and always try to have a positive attitude. People will see my smile; people will share their smiles. We will be grateful that we can see each other's smiles. Little did you ever think how much you took for granted. A smile can change your world. Life is full of opportunities and they are at our reach. We have the privilege, and we have the will to do it. We are blessed and we should thank God. Although God didn't send this illness to us he allowed it to happen for us to learn from it. This virus has a positive vein for us. It made us more appreciative of what we have and that is one of the best lessons we could ever learn. We are happier because we are more appreciative of what we have. God Bless.

CHAPTER SEVEN

Life is a mystery, live each day to the fullest.

Blessings

Life is a blessing as if we didn't already know that we certainly must now. We have had another tough lesson in life. It is called survival. We have been to the depths of finding our way out of this pandemic. We are on our way and a very positive way. I can feel in my heart and in my soul a breath of fresh air…clean, fresh air. Doesn't that sound wonderful? We now have vaccines, and we are getting vaccinated. We are going to get rid of this devil that lives amongst us and it will feel our wrath. God is good and He has given the doctors and the scientist the knowledge to create a powerful vaccine. Set your sites on a beautiful new year. Barbecues (cookouts) to us in New England, eating outside, inside with our loved ones and friends, going to movies, concerts, etc. BUT most of all we can be with family and friends. We can hug them, and we can kiss them we can see them. We can all be happy and we all can be safe. God bless America and the world. Amen.

Life Is a Blessing

I think about how far I have come in sharing my thoughts, feelings, and love. I have always wanted to share the beauty one feels when giving part of themselves to help others. Have you ever had a bad day when there wasn't anything that was going right? The weather was even dreary. You're not feeling as well as you had hoped, you just didn't feel. What could brighten your day? How do you feel when you see someone smile at you? Do you feel a sense of acceptance, a feeling of love, and a feeling of being cared about, all because of a smile? This doesn't cost anything and however, it gave you everything. A reason to begin your day with a smile on yourself.

The day has just begun so it is up to you how you are going to live your day. Remember it is your day. If you wake up feeling good that is a very good start. Keep that feeling in your heart. If you wake up feeling not so good there is always something you can do to make it better. One free thing is your attitude. Say to yourself, "Okay not a great day but I can make the best of it." Maybe you had plans to go out with a friend. Maybe you wanted to take the day for yourself and do something you have been wanting to do. However, you now have to tell your self-plan A is not going to work for me today. So, you go to plan B. Remember you have plan B. Maybe today you are supposed to rest. Maybe it is a sign from above letting you know that someone is looking after you. It is your attitude that is going to get you through this tough day or not-so-tough day.

Each day is a blessing, and we all have a lot to be thankful for. Do you have a family that loves you? Are you able to work? Are you able to get outside on your own? Take a walk, ride a bike, drive a car? Do you have friends that you can talk to? Can you read? Can you write? These are just a few things that you can. Be thankful for that. Focus on one thing for the day and make it your mission, your goal. You can do it. When you focus on something else than focusing on not feeling your best your mind takes you away from that place. You will feel better before you know it. I know that you are thinking easier said than done. This is true but whoever said that life was easy. It is what we make of it.

Loneliness is a sad affair and feeling empty is not a good way to feel it. We need to feel good inside and feel good out. We can do this without a lot of work. We just have to believe. I do believe in a positive attitude. Attitude is 90%. So, as I talk about a positive attitude, I would like to mention that sometimes it is difficult to keep our chin up and see a positive view out of a very frustrating situation. So, here is my story on a very important issue that I would like to share with all of you. I am sure you will read this and relate.

So as this day passes, I am writing during the worldwide Pandemic. It is not very pretty here in Massachusetts. However, it is dark and gloomy and it feels like there is no hope. BUT, there is hope, there always is hope even if it feels like there is just a thread of hope. Mostly everyone is trying to sign up for a Covid 19 shot. I remember the first day at 8:00 am when the website opened for us in Massachusetts the website crashed. Everyone that morning, of course, logged onto the computer to get the very few shots they had before anyone else. The telephone number you could call had an over two-hour wait only to be told there was nothing left at the time. I remember I was put on a "callback" list with no concrete answer when they may call. The problem was you need to be able to answer the phone when they call you back. What happens when you can't answer at the time they call you? You cannot call them back with a return phone call. I must say this entire process was so frustrating. There just has to be another way. So, this is how it is.

My personal feeling is I feel the doctors' offices should have the vaccine. This is a crisis in the world and there had to be a better way. I am praying and I am hoping that they do find an alternative measure to straighten this out. I know the two vaccines need to be frozen and kept in freezers. So, I wonder why that doctors' offices can't rent freezers to solve that issue. The new vaccine Johnson and Johnson just got approved today (March 1, 2021). This vaccine doesn't need to be frozen and is a one-time shot. How positive is that? There is always a positive thread. So, with all of this going on I will not lose my faith and hope. So how do I keep positive with all of this? Okay, this is how I am dealing with it.

Okay, eventually we will all get the Covid 19 vaccine shot. It may not be as quick as we want it, but we will get it. So, I say to myself. Many people somehow are lucky enough to have already gotten it. God bless them. If so, we can look at it this way for now. The many people who have gotten the Covid shot make us less likely to contract the virus because the contagion is diminishing. Spring is just around the corner and it is getting warmer. People will be doing things outside. People will still be wearing their masks, washing their hands, and keeping their distance. So, if I combine all those measures we have to relax and know that when it is time for us it will work out for us. I do believe that God does have a time for us that is best to get the Covid 19 vaccine.

We need to work on patience and put trust in God our savior to enlighten and remind us that He is right beside us all the way. I know this but sometimes I need to give myself a boost. I need to keep my faith and remain positive. There is a vaccine we didn't have too long ago. The doctors and the scientist are working hard to improve it all the time.

There is always a reason for anything that may happen. So even though searching the web endlessly hasn't been too positive we turn our thinking around make it the best it can be. So, to all of you out there don't ever give up. This will all work out for us.

We will look back and say Amen to the end of a nightmare for all of us in the entire world. We always wake up from a nightmare and it is always better.

Next time you are out taking a walk, strolling in a mall, or whatever you are doing smile at someone. You may never know what this person is going through, but you lifted their spirits and cheered them. Life goes on and everyone in today's world can use a smile and a hug and someday soon we will be back to our hugging that we all miss so very much in today's world.

So, I extend to all of you a gigantic beautiful loving smile. I hope you pass it on, and I wish you a beautiful day.

I close this chapter with a poem straight from my heart.

Life Is a Mystery

Life is a mystery if we didn't know before,
It brings unexpected issues that are hard to endure.
We look at the picture and say what we can do
We pray to our God for an answer so true.
We never give up and we look for the best
For attitude is 90%
We have nothing to lose and all to save by
Keeping positive we have all to gain.
So tonight when you go to bed keep your
Eyes closed and say a little prayer.
To thank our Lord for what we have and
Remain faithful and ever grateful.
So I send you blessings from above and pray
That you will hear their love without delay.
Sending you the angels that will watch
And protect you, along with your loved ones will
Stay close beside you. Amen

Life is a mystery live each day to the fullest

What are your thoughts?

Life is full of surprises and we never know which way the tide will turn. The mystery of the ocean will always be intriguing to me. We look at the ocean and deep within its ocean blue, I wonder what is underneath.

The secret it holds within its depths.

CHAPTER EIGHT

Have you ever carried with you an umbrella to block the sun or have you only carried an umbrella to block the rain?

The Year 2020

Did the year 2020 give you a **"2020"** eye vision view of our world? Did **"2020"** Open our Eyes, Our Mind, Our Hearts, Our souls? Do we view things in a clearer vision? Do we see things differently with an open and clear mind? What matters most to us? What is most important to us? So many questions. I know for myself I appreciate life so much more. I thought, I always did! However, the year 2020 told me "you had no idea what you had" I guess I didn't! I hope this lesson will be just that "a lesson." It is up to us to wake up and pay attention. If we don't learn from our mistakes, they remain mistakes and we will remain stuck in this horrible world of illness, stress, and much uneasiness. If we learn from this it will become, I feel, the most valuable lesson we have experienced. So, the year 2021 opens to us a brand-new world. We will have a new beginning. We will have a new start to begin what matters most to us and how important it is to us putting into use what we have learned. So, I say smile a big smile because it will be a different world, but it will be a better world and we will be happy. To quote a saying "This is the first day of our lives." Blessings AMEN!

Umbrella

Today, we are living under an Umbrella. This Umbrella is the Covid 19 virus. It isn't nice but it is ruthless and relentless. It is an evil fighter. As you all know an umbrella has many spokes. I will use this analogy to focus on what I would like to share. No one is exempt from this horrific virus that is plaguing the world. There isn't a race, religion, State, Country, Continent, or this earth is exempt from feeling the effects of this. Rather than look at the big picture (the umbrella) let's take each spoke and see how it can be woven into positive spokes rather than destructive ones.

First, let's look at the handle of the umbrella. The base of the umbrella is the strongest. It is where it gets its strength. It is the core. It is the firm foundation that makes the spokes stronger than the black veil that encompasses us today. We all live different lives. No one has lived our lives, so we see things differently in some sense. Some of us have immediate families, so have families outside of our immediate. Some of us have ourselves and no family. We are family. Some of us pray and some of us don't. Some of us have positive attitudes and some of us have negative one. We live our lives how we were taught to live our lives. WE have a choice to change that if it doesn't feel right in our gut. How we react to what life deals us is what will make our lives happy or sad. We have a choice. We are given the right to choose whatever steps we need to take.

How do you react to a stressful situation? Let's look at:

Spoke # 1. For me, it is my family. I in my opinion am blessed to have a loving, caring family who loves me with all their heart and soul. I in return love them back. This keeps the umbrella in a positive light. What is your Spoke #1? I am sure you can find a positive.

Spoke # 2. For me it is my friends, Friends are important to me, very important. Each of my friends sheds light on me. We care for each other and we matter to each other. We are there for each other. I love them all.

Spoke # 3. For me, it is my Health. My health is not great, but it could be a lot worse. I am a cancer survivor...Years ago I was given less than a year to live but I am here typing away and hoping I reach each and every one of you. I lost my hearing in one ear due to a virus, but I can still hear from my other ear. I have a heart condition that was caused by the chemotherapy that I received to cure my cancer. However, I am alive and with great doctors, I am surviving and my condition is under control. I am thankful for that. I can be completely independent and follow the guidelines for my health. So, the spoke isn't perfect, but do you see the strength in it. It made me stronger, and it made me not look back. Go forward is the way to go. Life isn't perfect so why would I even try to go there? I work with what I have and I am thankful for that.

Spoke #4. For me it is Freedom is a big one. I am sure it is for everybody. It is a gift. I treasure this. I can decide how I am going to live. I can make my own choices to do or not to do. I can choose where to live, share my thoughts, feelings, my views, or just say nothing at all. I have freedom in my life and best of all thanks to our servicemen it is free for all of us. I am thankful to the servicemen and I am thankful to God.

Spoke 5. For me, it is my Faith. I have to say the strongest spoke for me on my umbrella is my faith. My faith has always been my stronghold. It is my greatest gift. I do believe in life after we pass. We pass we don't die. Our body which is just a casing dies but our soul lives on and never dies. Knowing that God is more powerful than anything or any person place or thing is enormous. God gives us a choice to make decisions. God does not send things or make things happen. God gave us a mind to make decisions. We make the choice and sometimes it is not the right choice. We make our bed. He doesn't send illness, violence, bad weather, or anything that isn't good. He is ALL good. He allows things to happen because He doesn't interfere with our choices. I know when I need help, I pray. I believe that he answers my prayers. I always say God's will be done. Sometimes I pray for something that isn't right for me so I end my prayers with: "God's will be done" Amen.

Spoke #6 Love is my greatest gift. I feel blessed with love in my heart and soul. I have always loved my family, friends, acquaintances, and people in general. I have always had a desire to help others and to help them feel better about themselves, and to help them have a more positive attitude rather than a negative attitude. I believe God gave me this gift. Helping others be able to look at life through a positive lens rather than a negative one is what I have always wanted to do. This has always been one of my goals. This is so important in every day of life, especially in today's world.

So, this is my umbrella. Each of you has your own umbrella. What does your umbrella look like today? If it is as bright as it can be - Congratulations!

If not, you can change it. Remember you have a free choice and you can do it. I have faith in you, my dear friends.

Remember never to give up. There is always hope even if it is just a thread of hope.

A little Poem to make you smile:

Beautiful Umbrella
{Open or Shut}

Beautiful Umbrella what color are you today,
Are you a bright red or gloomy gray?
You can open or shut on a rainy day or open and shut on a bright sunny day.
See beautiful Umbrella you can have your way, it up to you which way you want to sway.
So remember the weather if it's sunny or gray,
You always have a choice to make your day.

CHAPTER NINE

*Never give up. There is always hope,
even if it is just "A Thread of Hope"*

Blessings to All

2021 will bring a new beginning to all of us. It has been a big wake-up year. Have we been asleep, unappreciative, taking things for granted, going along our way whichever way we wanted? I can honestly say that for most of us we have to answer yes to all or most of these questions. We have taken things for granted. I don't think we will do that again. We will be forever aware and reminded of what we all went through. We will be able to sit where we worship and be ever so thankful that we can be there and pray and praise God. We will be able to sit in a restaurant and look around take a deep breath and be thankful that we can do that again. We will go to a beach and be able to smell the fresh air with ease. We will walk through a mall, sit at a pavilion, sit in a movie theater, go to a concert, and live our lives like we had known it to be. We will be free, free at last, and hopefully so grateful. Where do we begin to thank all who have helped us get here? I first thank

God. Thank you, God, for inspiring and giving the knowledge to the countless workers who helped us get to our "new" world. Thank you, doctors, scientists, nurses, health care workers, pharmacists, grocery workers, and so many more that I have not mentioned, but not forgotten. As I write this, three vaccines have been approved, they have proven to be effective, safe, and available to all shortly. This is our HOPE. We have a lifeline and hopefully, we will all grab onto it. It is our future into a brand-new world. A world where we are all stronger, braver, wiser. Grateful. But most of all thankful that we all have another chance to live our lives more fully. I thank my God and all of you who worked endlessly to cure the world in more ways than one. God Bless America and the world. Love and Blessings. Jacqui DeLorenzo

Blessings for 2021

If we were to start counting our blessings what would be the first blessing that you would choose? I would say for me it would be my health. I have always been thankful for my health especially now as this virus is hitting all of us right in the face. If you don't have your health what do you have?

One could have all the money in the world, but it won't buy you your health. As I look back through my past years, I have had issues with my health.

We have all had our health issues. Some of us have had more than others but I am sure we all have some to share. Many of these illnesses are out of our control. However, it is in our control how we are going to handle what we are going to do with it, how we are going to handle it. We do have control over that. I want you to hold on to that friends. It gives you power, it gives you strength, it gives you a good feeling inside. You are in control and remember you are the captain of your ship.

As I mentioned before I am a cancer survivor who was given less than a year to live. I was only 27 years old when I got the devastating news. I had a very rare (7 in the world) type of cancer. It was a tumor in my leg. They thought of removing my leg. However, since I had such a short time to live, they decided to let me keep my leg. Praise God for that. I can thank my doctors for not rushing into amputating my leg in some hope they may be able to save me. It was a miracle that the doctor who was familiar with the other rare cases had just been transferred to Mass General hospital two weeks before I ended up in the hospital. He worked with my primary care, chemotherapist, and radiologist to find a treatment that would work for me. It was a tough treatment that I would not wish on my worst enemy, but I made it through and here I am today writing to you all. What held me on, what made me not give up, what helped me still smile? It was the "hope" I hung on to. It was my faith and belief in my savior. It was the trust I had in the doctors. It was my optimism; I chose to be a conqueror and not be a victim. I remember asking myself "Am I going to let evil win over me?"

Why would I do that? Why would I let "evil" win? No way would I let that happen. I was going to fight this until the bitter end, and I was going to win!!! I can't say that at times I felt I was losing the battle but very often I was lifted by my inner spirit. The best part of this entire struggle that I went through was that I won the War!!!

So, as you look at your life be thankful for your health. If you do not have the best of health be thankful for what you do have. I believe that in one's life with all its tragedies, health issues, injustice, and personal concerns we still have a choice to be a victim or a conqueror. I think we all want to be a conqueror and not let evil lurk in our lives. I just survived bladder cancer and just got diagnosed with GIST cancer. We were born with free will. We have a choice, and the choice is ours.

CHAPTER TEN

*May the blessing of the day sit on your shoulder
for it is God who has placed it there.*

A Hole in the Sidewalk

Have you ever fallen into a hole?

I remember reading the poem: "There's a Hole in the Sidewalk" by Portia Nelson. This blog was inspired by that poem.

Sometimes we keep falling into the same hole. We feel depressed. Still, we walk down the same sidewalk, but we begin to realize we don't want to be there. However, we don't take charge of it, we don't want to own it. But is it a habit?

Do we walk down the same sidewalk repeatedly falling into a deep dark hole?? Why do we do this?

Well, often the devil we know is better than the devil we don't know attitude. It is easy to be stuck. This lets us fall into this negative path. Is this a positive way to feel or relate to our fears--NO of course not? We need to avoid that sidewalk. So, what can we do?

We look at how can we change, feel better, by charting our path to a new walk. There are many sidewalks. We can change our path. We can take a positive path. We need to walk down a different sidewalk. It is our choice.

I am not saying it is always easy but when you make that change you will feel uplifted and gain more confidence because you did it!!

Don't fret if you don't accomplish this overnight. You didn't get where you are overnight. You will get there! You may walk down the sidewalk and look into the hole, but you don't fall in, you may walk around it. This is okay, it is a process.

So, we need to be the captain and focus on a rainbow, a flower, a happy thought, a dream, a wish, focus on a positive route. We need to make a positive change in what we are stuck in. Even if it is small, we need to make this step. Our attitude and focus are on feeling better and skipping the negative sidewalk. We walk down a different sidewalk completely and find our rainbow, a flower, a happy thought, etc.

Keep the faith and look forward. You did it!!

Coping in Today's World

Cope is another strong four-letter word. How are you coping in today's world? It is certainly a different world, isn't it? For most of us, it is a world we have never experienced. We all live our own lives no one truly knows what we are going through and how we truly feel. We often hear, "I know how you feel" but they don't. They didn't live your life, have your feelings or thoughts. However, one may know how it feels to lose someone, lose a job, be sick. I think that is why we sometimes find it difficult to understand others and the way they cope with life's difficulties.

We all handle stress differently. I feel sometimes this world is surreal.

I could never understand how someone could feel pleasure in hurting others. Of course, this is my heart talking. I know in the reality that the individual is a very unhappy person and can only deal with their stress by hurting others so they don't feel alone. They think they feel better by making someone else feel lower than they feel. It is sad but it is true. This is a negative way that some people handle stress. Unfortunately, this doesn't make them feel better at all. It is so negative that they feel worse about themselves. This keeps them in a negative state of unhappiness. It is sad how someone can get in that state of being.

I was very much abused as a child by my peers. I went to a catholic grammar school from grade three to grade eight. The kids were brutal to me. They physically, mentally, and emotionally abused me. I lived in fear and to me, there was no escape. Some kids threatened to hurt my mom. I stayed home to protect her. I feared for her life. I feared for my siblings and me that we would be left alone without a mom. My dad was not in the picture so we would have no one to help us. We would lose our mommy. I wanted to end my life because I was so depressed and so very sad. I could not understand at the time why they were being so mean and so nasty to me. It is funny so to speak but I never fought back. I could never hurt them the way they were hurting me. Even as a child I did not want them to feel the pain I was feeling. I just put up with it and tried a way to cope. So how did a young teen cope? Inside my heart and my soul, I grabbed on to the hope that things would get better. Even though it was just a thread of hope I would not let go. I hung onto my faith. I knew Jesus loved me and I knew he would not leave me. I prayed every day and every night that Jesus would stay by my side and help me cope with each coming day. I entered a public high school and my life was better. I was away from the terrible kids that haunted me daily. I just wanted an out. I thank God for a new chance at finding some friends and being happy. I was a very sad kid. This was a great new start for me and my thread of hope inspired me to go on. I had a new start. I had a new school. I made new friends but not too many. I was too afraid that they would turn against me. I was cautious but would not let it stop me from trying. I had hope. I had hope for the future. I made a plan that I was going to help others any way I could that felt the kind of pain I felt. I wanted to help them to know that they are special and that they matter in the world. I wanted to save them from feeling the pain and hurt that I once felt. I wanted to set them free. It is so interesting today because even though I needed to still work on my self-esteem I still had the will, and I had the way to do it. It meant everything to me to help those that felt so alone, lonely, unloved, and so sad.

We all must find the way that works best for us. This isn't always easy. We all need to take control of our lives and be optimistic in how we follow our path. I do believe however that we are born with certain strengths and certain weaknesses. However, this does not mean that even though some things are more difficult than others that we can't make it through and reach the end with a positive end. As we work on our weaknesses, we get stronger and stronger. We build up confidence and we gain control of our lives. I feel we all have hidden coping skills that we aren't even aware of. I can't cope is the wrong thing to say or think. You have to draw on your positive attitude and say" I can cope." And I can and will do it. As a child, I always wrote poems, thoughts, feelings in journals that I kept forever. This was one of my coping skills. This is one of the things that I did that helped me cope with all the negativity in my life at the time. For me, it was a relief and it kept me most of the time from feeling so low about how I felt. I would love to share a coping poem with you.

Sometimes just reading or hearing words from a positive uplifting poem could be the key that could save your life.

COPE

Coping is something we all can do.
Sometimes it's more difficult but we have the tools.
We pull on the strength that is within us all and we
Will step ahead and win the war.

Life is full of circumstances that are
Good and bad but it is how we cope that makes us last.
So how do we start when it is already there we look inside
And we begin the ride.

Life is never a real smooth ride
It is often like a Roller coaster with unknown stride.
It has ups
And downs and fast and slow and often turns in a space
We don't know.

So this is where Cope goes along,
With Hope to keep us going and hanging on.
We have a choice
So why wouldn't we choose one of the best skills we were
born with.

How did you feel reading "COPE"?

Was it just words to you or did it resonate with you? Did it make you think about searching your soul and finding that inner peace that will help you strive through what you must? Living our life every day is inevitable. So how do we begin? We should get up in the morning and start our day with one step forward looking up. We should not look back for what does that does. We don't look ahead because what does that do. We have no guarantee of that either. We should live one day at a time. We should make the best of what life has given to us that day. This is all part of coping and dealing with the day. As we build up our positivity, we get stronger. Our plate begins to be filled with positive things, positive attitudes, and great coping skills. Look at your life as a giant platter. What are you going to place on that plate?

Are you looking at a flowery plate or are you looking at that plate as a dark, dreary, unwelcoming plate? Once again, we have a choice. One thing that God has given to all of us is the freedom to choose how we are going to handle life's struggles, happiness, rights, or wrongs, being kind, helpful, being cruel, and selfish. We and we alone have that choice. It is ours to own. I know that I chose my life to help others and be as kind and gentle as I can. I feel better inside my heart. I know what it is like to have been dealt unkind, and cruel too. I would never want anybody to feel that pain. I wish I had a magic want that I could waive to make everyone happy, everyone is nice, kind, and helpful, and so forth. I wish I could give them the beautiful spirit that I feel within me. You have to allow yourself to let go. You can't be afraid it is just a beautiful place to be. What a beautiful world this would be.

As I close this chapter, I hope you found it to be helpful in some way. We all need help, we all need friends, we all need caring and we, in turn, need to care for others. We are going through a tough time, but we will make it. We will be strong, more caring, more loving, more grateful, and more appreciative for what we have, and we will be happier in our lives.

Poems to Warm Your Heart

Angel Love

May the angels always guide your way through life.
May you feel their love from above.

They will show you the way if you invite them in
As you pray throughout the day.
They won't come in unless you ask, they respect you
All the time. You will always feel their love
My friend. They are always will be by your side.

Life has Meaning

Life is full of meaning and we never know its turns
But there always is a reason for what
happens and we learn

Sometimes it's very happy and enriches our life so sweet.
And sometimes it turns sour and challenges us to meet.

We are stronger than a warrior and we fight until the end
For we are strong with God's great grace and we will
surely win.

In Memory of my dear friend Nancy

A Friend in Heaven

So in my heart, you will always be, and safely you will
stay until the day we meet again:
I'll keep you in my prayers.

I often reminisce about all the times we had, the laughter
and the fun we had, and the things just you and I shared.

You left such a great legacy with your strength of never
giving up; we all were so very proud of you and loved you
with all our hearts.

You left two beautiful children Jennifer and Kate, who
were the precious diamonds you loved with all your heart.

Your loving husband Paul who you always loved and admired who loved you with all his heart and will always keep you in his heart.

And now dear friend Nancy, your journey on earth has ended. But I know you're looking down on us and sending us your love.

So my tribute to you my dear friend is the never-ending love for I will always have you deep within my heart.

I invite you to check out my website:
jacquidelorenzo.com
May your life be blessed with everything beautiful!
Be happy you are only here once so make the best of it.

BE HAPPY

EPILOGUE

When you wake up in the morning how are you feeling? The day has just begun so it is up to you how you choose to live it. If you wake up feeling good that is a very good start. Keep the feeling of good in your heart and soul. If you wake up feeling not so good there is something you can do to make it better. Remember you are the captain and don't forget that. My second book "Straight from my Heart" is a collection of true stories that will warm your heart. I also included poems written from my heart. You will find the stories in *"Straight from my Heart"* book not only mine but of other people just like you. Reading an uplifting book will be a sure way to help you. The messages will lift your spirits and help you have a great attitude towards life and the day ahead of you. I was always a journal-keeper, and this lifted my spirits. This is what inspired me to write my experiences to share and help others. It helped save me from a tough day that I "knew" was ahead of me. *A Thread of Hope* is another book that I wrote mainly to help others never give up. No matter how low you can feel in a day there is always another day that will be better. The day you are feeling low hang do something to help you through the day. Don't dwell on negative thoughts, find a positive thought. Hanging on to that thread of hope if that is how you feel, can be your saving grace. There is always a positive spoke in your life. Do you have a family, a loved one that is in your bubble? Are you able to get up in the morning day and even make yourself a cup of coffee/tea? Can you take a nice walk? Even smile more during the day even if you don't feel like it. It's catchy. These are just a few simple things that help you with a better attitude. A negative attitude will lead you no wear except depression. Who needs that? Not me!! It is being thankful for what we have instead of what we don't have. I learned through my own life that I am positive because of my spirituality. My faith and my belief in Jesus have helped my positive attitude in life. Each of you must find what works best for you. Thank you so much to every one of you for all your love and support. I am so grateful to you all. You have helped me in more ways than you know by reading my blogs. I write them in hopes that it will reach others and help them in any way they need "A Thread of Hope" and this is "Straight from my Heart." Love and Blessings

www.ingramcontent.com/pod-product-compliance
Lightning Source LLC
LaVergne TN
LVHW020431080526
838202LV00055B/5120